Cultivating Communities Series

The Shape of Our Lives

A Field Guide for Congregational Formation

<blockquote>
Philip D. Kenneson

Debra Dean Murphy

Jenny C. Williams

Stephen E. Fowl

James W. Lewis
</blockquote>

ENGLEWOODPRESS.COM

Published by Englewood Press
57 North Rural Street.
Indianapolis, IN 46201

www.englewoodpress.com

ISBN 978-1-934406-17-5 (digital)
ISBN 978-1-934406-18-2 (print)

Library of Congress Control Number: 2024947508

Cover design: Eliza Whyman

Table of Contents

The Cultivating Communities Series

Our human bodies bear witness to the truth of our lives: to the many sorts of care we have given them or to joys and traumas that they have survived. Similarly, social bodies also bear witness. They take the shape of their members' desires, convictions, and stories. And our churches are no exception. Ideally, our congregations will take a shape that bears witness to the life, death, resurrection, and teachings of Jesus. But all too often that witness is distorted by other loves and other desires in the midst of church communities that don't look a whole lot like Jesus of Nazareth. Nationalism and greed are two such loves that dilute and distort the Christian witness of churches.

In an age dominated by deep social divides – between the political right and left; between rich and poor; between various racial and ethnic identities, between generations; and between educational backgrounds, to name just a few – how is it even possible that a church might have any shape at all beyond the nearly amorphous form taken by the loose network of her individual members?

Beyond these deep divides and the existential threat they pose to our congregations, I am hopeful churches can still mature into the full stature of a body that bears a striking resemblance to Jesus. This maturing is a slow process that will not only take time but also hard work and intentionality. What shape will our individual bodies take if we neglect to care for their physical and mental well-being? Similarly, our churches must be attentive to tending and cultivating our life together, seeking day-by-day, month-by-month, and year-by-year to more fully embody Jesus together in our particular place. This work of patient cultivation lies at the heart of **congregational formation.**

In many ways the contours of congregational formation parallel those of personal spiritual formation. Both congregational and personal formation are driven by the desire to more fully know and embody Jesus, and both take the shape of intentional practices that serve to form us into Christlikeness. However, congregational formation can be particularly messy because it requires the alignment of the desires of multiple people, not just one person. Efforts to align desires by emotional manipulation, or by more authoritarian tactics, will undoubtedly fail with time because their means are decidedly *not* those of the patient love and compassion of Jesus. In these cases, formation does happen, but the shape that is emerging looks little like Jesus.

Indeed, congregational formation occurs as we learn to be attentive to God's presence in us and among us in the Holy Spirit. We learn through a multitude of practices, especially conversation, to share our convictions, our hopes, and our stories together. And we learn to receive one another with gratitude as a vital means of God's provision for shaping and sustaining our life together. Just as our personal bodies constantly adapt, discern, mature, and move through the world as an intricate network of conversations, so also conversation becomes the way that our churches discern together who our members are, how we will care for our collective body, and how we strive to embody Christ together in ways that our neighbors see and become curious about the way of Jesus.

This new Cultivating Communities Series of books serves to offer churches tools for the long journey of congregational formation. These books are intended as field guides to help orient your congregation through essential conversations on this journey. This series is the fruit of a collaborative effort between Cultivating Communities (an initiative designed to assist churches in the work of congregational formation, based at Englewood Christian Church in Indianapolis), Missio Alliance, and the Ekklesia Project. Cultivating Communities is funded by a grant from the Lilly Endowment's Thriving Congregations Initiative, and a portion of this generous funding has been used to launch this new series of books.

The first book in this series, *The Shape of Our Lives*, is a revised and updated edition of a resource originally produced in 2008 by the Ekklesia Project, which introduces the key elements and dynamics of congregational formation. Written by a team of pastors and theological/biblical scholars, including Phil Kenneson, Deborah Dean Murphy, Jenny Williams, Stephen Fowl, and James Lewis, *The Shape of Our Lives* will serve not only as a primer on congregational formation, but also a theological backdrop for the subsequent books in this series. Look for this first book to be available in October 2024.

Building upon our conviction that conversation is the central practice of congregational formation, the second book in this series (*The Virtue of Dialogue*) recounts the earliest years of Englewood Christian Church's journey of learning to grow together in conversation. We hope this story will provide imagination for many churches about how they might learn to talk and grow together within their own particular contexts.

Subsequent volumes in the series will address specific key facets of congregational formation, including how to read scripture together, how to think and talk about money in our congregations, and more. Each volume will incorporate discussion questions intended to spark conversation. Although each book can be read and reflected on by individual church leaders, this series is primarily intended to be read, prayed over, and discussed by groups within a congregation, including perhaps in some settings, the congregation as a whole. We hope the very form of these books is consistent with and serves to cultivate vital congregational conversations.

C. Christopher Smith
Series Editor

Cultivating Communities Series Partners

Cultivating Communities is a growing network of congregational cohorts across North America, each composed of churches that are seeking to be conversant with the way of Jesus in their respective places. Our team is committed to journeying with congregations who desire to cultivate a deeper life together in Christ, which overflows into tangible love for the communities in which they are embedded.

Funded by a grant from the Lilly Endowment's Thriving Congregations Initiative, Cultivating Communities offers helpful resources and relationships for congregations to do the hard work of maturing into real communities that care about everything that is essential and necessary for sharing a common life together. Learn more at **CultivatingCommunities.com.**

The Ekklesia Project is a community of Christians from across the ecclesial spectrum who have found life-giving friendship through a shared hope in the vision of God's good shalom. In the early 2000s, the Ekklesia Project launched the Congregational Formation Initiative (CFI) to nurture and support congregations committed to making lifelong formation and discipleship central to their life together. One CFI participant described their experience in this program: "CFI has caused me to think seriously about what a church's role should be: not just a place to go for worship, studies, weddings, and funerals, but a dynamic community of forgiveness, reconciliation, and shalom inside and outside our walls."

This book was originally published by the Ekklesia Project as a resource for congregations in the CFI. This revised edition is published as a joint venture between Cultivating Communities and The Ekklesia Project. Find the Ekklesia Project online at **EkklesiaProject.org.**

Foreword

In a world where speed, productivity, and constant activity are often equated with success, many of us find ourselves yearning for something deeper and more enduring. The journey toward meaningful engagement with our communities and the cultivation of healthy congregations feels more urgent now than ever. This revised and updated version of *The Shape of Our Lives*, originally published in 2008, offers both a challenge and a guide to what it means to be the church in today's complex landscape.

Its focus on the essential nature of congregational formation is integral to the Cultivating Communities initiative, a project Missio Alliance is privileged to collaborate on alongside Englewood Christian Church. Our shared goal is to help congregations flourish by providing the tools and insights needed to navigate today's challenges. This book aligns perfectly with our vision of congregational health and vitality, making it a valuable resource for pastors and church leaders.

More than merely a collection of ideas, *The Shape of Our Lives* is an invitation to slow down, reflect, and reimagine what it means to be the church in today's world. Through the lens of personal and congregational formation, the authors challenge us to examine the desires that drive our actions, discern the convictions that guide our trust, and reflect on the character we exhibit in our walk with God. They encourage us to explore the stories that have shaped us and to be open to the new stories God is writing in our midst. This exploration is not just an intellectual exercise; it's a call to recognize that formation is a communal journey, deeply rooted in the stories we share, the practices we embody, and the institutions that shape our collective existence.

As someone who has dedicated much of my life to fostering holistic approaches to faith and mission, I find the principles laid out in this book both inspiring and actionable. *The Shape of Our Lives* offers churches a roadmap for engaging with the complexities of our time, urging us to embrace a vision of intentional formation, rooted in a deep understanding of who we are and what we are called to be as the body of Christ. I trust that as you journey through these pages, you will find both the inspiration and the tools necessary to help your congregation flourish in today's world.

Lisa Rodriguez-Watson, National Director, Missio Alliance and contributing author to *Red Skies: 10 Essential Conversations Exploring Our Future as the Church*; *Voices of Lament: Reflections on Brokenness and Hope in a World Longing for Justice*; and *The Least of These: Practicing a Faith Without Margins*.

Missio Alliance is a Managing Partner in the Cultivating Communities initiative. Founded in 2011, Missio Alliance offers in-depth theological and practical direction for the many pastors and church leaders attempting to navigate the challenges of ministry in a culturally dynamic, post-Christianizing era. Learn more at **MissioAlliance.org.**

Introduction: What is Congregational Formation?

This field guide is designed to foster important conversations within the life of congregations and parishes. The church in our day needs to think carefully and discuss openly what it means to be the church. Numerous forces are pressing in on congregations, including cultural shifts that nudge them to the margins of North American society and deep sociopolitical divides that are splitting them apart. Although church attendance was declining for years before the COVID-19 pandemic in 2020, it dropped off more rapidly during and after the pandemic. Although many churches and denominations have shifted politically to the right or the left due to their official policies on social issues like same-sex marriages, most local congregations still contain a robust mix of perspectives on social issues. These varied perspectives threaten to divide many congregations, and color their members' views on crucial theological and practical questions central to that church's identity.

Just as it's difficult to imagine how a business, school, or athletic team could accomplish its purpose if participants had very different and possibly competing understandings of what that purpose was, so it is with the church. If the church gathers each week with vastly different and competing understandings of what it means to be a compassionate and flourishing community, it's hard to imagine that things will go well.

This book explores the many ways formation is always happening whether we are aware of it or not, and its guiding assumption is twofold: First, the church is called to be a community of formation; and second, this calling is always lived out in particular social contexts where other kinds of formation are also taking place. Are we aware of how our lives are being shaped simply by living everyday life in the ways society encourages and rewards? Are we aware of the ways the cultural formation we undergo may be at odds with our call to be formed into the image of Christ? It's one thing to *acknowledge in the abstract* that we are always being shaped and formed by the world around us; it's quite another to consider deeply how this may be taking place in very particular ways in our daily lives.

We want to encourage congregations to develop or strengthen habits of attending carefully to their life together. You can tell a great deal about a congregation by examining its conversational habits. When people in a congregation get together, *what* do they talk about? Are they able to talk about things that really matter (and are therefore potentially dangerous), or is all or most of their conversation about safe topics such as the weather and sports? And if a congregation has developed the habit of talking about important but difficult matters, *how* are these conversations carried out? Is there anything about the way Christians engage in difficult conversations that is rooted in God's desire for the church, or do they go about these conversations largely as the surrounding culture does?

For this reason, the pages that follow are meant to assist in shared exploration, not to set a one-size-fits-all agenda. No one expects that once you finish this book you will have all the answers; rather, the hope is that you will have discovered together the importance of several defining questions around which you may orient your continuing journey to be a faithful community of disciples of Jesus Christ.

Some Working Assumptions

All of us have working assumptions that guide nearly everything we do. Sometimes we're quite conscious of these assumptions, though often we're not. You may find it helpful to know upfront some of the key working assumptions behind this text. Although there's no expectation that you will necessarily share all of these assumptions, we hope readers will at least see why some of these assumptions matter. Here are a few important ones:

- The Christian faith is not simply a set of beliefs or doctrines that one assents to with their mind, but an entire way of life animated by the Spirit of Jesus Christ.

- The church is a community of disciples called together to bear embodied witness to Jesus Christ, not least by being formed more and more into the image of Christ.

- Christian formation is always enabled and empowered by the Holy Spirit, yet it typically takes place through rather mundane human processes and activities.

- None of us has arrived; we are all pilgrims on the path of discipleship to fullness of life in Jesus Christ.

- Despite very real challenges and obstacles, the church in our day has good reasons to believe God's Spirit is alive and working in and through our congregations.

- The animating and life-giving work of God's Spirit is also always actively present and at work in the world beyond the confines of the church.

Worries about Formation Language

No discussion of formation can take place very long before some people get a little nervous. Is someone going to dictate what the shape of our lives is to be? Is someone going to suggest that faithfulness to Christ must look one particular way? Isn't there a real danger when people presume to form others?

In broaching this topic, we do well to avoid two extremes. At one end is what we might call the "cookie-cutter approach." This approach to formation insists it's relatively easy to spot the "real Christians," because they're the ones engaging in the behaviors "real Christians" engage in and avoiding behaviors that should be avoided. With this approach, formation primarily involves making sure everyone understands which behaviors are to be embraced and which ought to be avoided.

At the other extreme is what we might call the "hands-off approach." This approach insists very little, if anything, can or should be said definitively about the shape of Christian life. With this approach, any attempt to form people intentionally is regarded as an unwarranted imposition on people's freedom to shape their own personhood.

To its credit, the cookie-cutter approach rightly senses that we ought to be able to say *something* about how our lives should be affected by the good news of Jesus Christ. Is there really *no* reference point at all, no way to discern whether a particular person or community of persons is becoming more or less conformed to the image of Christ? To *its* credit, the hands-off approach is nervous about the ways in which this reference point has been defined in the past. Too often these lists of sanctioned or taboo behaviors have little connection to the good news of Jesus Christ.

Although on the surface these two extremes appear to be polar opposites, on a deeper level they are remarkably similar in at least one important respect: both largely presume what it means to be a Christian is primarily an *individual* affair. In the cookie-cutter approach, the individual is told what behaviors he or she needs to engage in (and avoid) to be considered a faithful Christian. In the hands-off approach, individuals are largely left to their own devices to figure this out, because no one else would presume to tell them what their lives should look like.

This book begins with a different understanding: Being a follower of Jesus is always a communal affair. Indeed, one of this book's primary purposes is to encourage congregations to develop more robust practices of communal discernment--to continually seek to understand how best to live out our shared calling to be a community of disciples in a particular time and place.

Hopes and Expectations

Readers will no doubt have their own hopes and expectations as they begin exploring congregational formation in their own contexts. In fact, it would be wise to articulate as many of these as possible in order to get a sense of what people hope will result from your communal discernments. Here are a few things we hope will happen as a result of your time and commitment:

- You will deepen your desire and your ability to reflect on the shape of your own life and the life of your congregation.

- You will deepen your desire and your abilities to discuss with other people matters that matter.

- As a congregation, you will develop a shared vocabulary as a tool to reflect upon and discuss together your common life.

- And finally, your conversations together would be used by God in some small way to deepen your shared practice of living out the gospel of Jesus Christ in your corner of God's world.

Here are some words of wisdom from congregations who have taken up the challenges of wrestling with formation in their own contexts:

- Be patient with all those involved in the conversation (including yourself!) and with the seemingly slow pace of congregational formation generally. Just as "Rome wasn't built in a day," neither are faithful congregations. The habits of thought and action that pose significant obstacles to faithful discipleship are firmly rooted in all of us because of years of formation. Examining these habits to discern how they are helping or hurting our life together as the church will require both time and a willingness to be uncomfortable. None of this will be easy, and there are no quick fixes or short cuts.

- Don't minimize what the Spirit may be doing *already* in your congregation as you gather to give careful consideration to your life together. Just because you don't see any tangible results right away doesn't mean the Spirit isn't working in your common life. Each time you gather, devote some time to celebrating the places where you do see the Spirit working in your life together and continue to trust God will bring to completion the good work begun in you.

- Finally, this resource is most beneficial when it is part of a larger practice of sharing life together. Many groups make studies such as these a part of a regular gathering where participants share a meal and their lives with each other. Many of the long-term benefits from these explorations come from intentionally connecting with people in your congregation on a deeper level.

One

Formation Happens!

O Lord, you are our Father;
we are the clay, and you are our potter;
we are all the work of your hand.
–Isaiah 64:8

I appeal to you therefore, brothers and sisters, by
the mercies of God, to present your bodies as a
living sacrifice, holy and acceptable to God,
which is your spiritual worship. Do not be con-
formed to this world, but be transformed by the
renewing of your minds, so that you may discern
what is the will of God—what is good and ac-
ceptable and perfect.
–Romans 12:1-2

Don't let the world squeeze you into its mold.
–Romans 12:2 (J. B. Phillips)

Whether we know it or not, or whether we acknowledge it or not, we are always being formed. We are always being molded. We are always being shaped. In short: formation happens.

In this respect, human beings are a bit like playdough: made in such a way that our lives are incredibly malleable, capable of being formed and shaped in any number of different ways. Presumably, God could have created human beings less like playdough and more like rocks. Had God done so, we would have arrived on the scene in a far more fixed and finished state.

Even though God made us capable of being shaped in any number of ways, this shouldn't be taken to imply that God doesn't care what shape we take. On the contrary, God desires that our lives take a certain shape, a certain form. Scripture tells us God desires that our lives be conformed to the image of Christ (Romans 8:29; 2 Corinthians 3:18). Indeed, 2 Peter suggests that the ultimate goal of God's work in our lives is to enable us to be "participants of the divine nature" (2 Peter 1:4). In this important respect, therefore, all Christians have the same calling: to be conformed to the image of Christ. All of us have been called to have our lives shaped and formed according to the pattern we see in Jesus. C. S. Lewis once insisted that the church exists for no other reason than to form persons into "little Christs" (which is what the word "Christian" literally means, after all). Indeed, Lewis went on to insist that if the church is not doing this, then "all the cathedrals, clergy, missions, sermons, even the Bible itself, are simply a waste of time".[1]

Yet, as already suggested, God's desire is not simply that we be conformed to the image of Christ. If that was all God desired, God could have created us as already finished sculptures. But God didn't do this, presumably because God desires that *we desire* to be so conformed and to open ourselves up to that transformation. God cannot force us to love God or to desire to be like God any more than one of us can force another person to love us or want to be like us. To coerce love is to violate its very nature. So Christian formation is first about right desire, about being open to the transformation possible in and through Jesus Christ and the work of the Spirit.

As the Body of Christ, the church is called to bear the imprint, the pattern, the image of Christ, just as a piece of playdough held tightly in your palms bears the imprint, the pattern, the image of your hands. Now human formation is, of course, much more complicated than picking up a piece of playdough and fashioning it into whatever strikes your fancy at the moment. Perhaps one of the most important differences is that our lives are being formed by many, many different factors. It's as if multiple hands are working on the

---

[1] Lewis, C.S. (2001). *Mere Christianity.* (Revised and Enlarged Ed.) Harper San Francisco.

playdough ball that is our life, often at the same time, and often with different purposes in mind. So if we feel as though our lives are being pulled and twisted in different directions, there's good reason for that: they are being pulled and twisted in different directions!

Consider just one example. One of the principal virtues of contemporary society is ambition. We are told in countless subtle and not-so-subtle ways that if you want to succeed in life, you must order your life in such a way that you are always calculating how to get ahead, how to ensure you are constantly advancing toward the top. When we attend to these pressures—these hands on our lump of dough—we find ourselves being formed to think and act in certain ways. We are encouraged to think of our co-workers in certain ways; we are led to think of our work's purpose in certain ways; we are even inclined to think of the direction and purpose of our entire lives in certain ways.

But what happens when those of us who are being so formed gather as the church on a particular Sunday morning and hear the Philippians 2:3-4 read: "Do nothing from selfish ambition or conceit, but in humility regard others as better than yourselves. Let each of you look not to your own interests, but to the interests of others."

How are we supposed to negotiate these different expectations? How are we supposed to be formed into the image of the humble Christ when the world around us is trying to squeeze us into its ambitious mold? Now perhaps these seemingly different pressures, voices, and agendas can be brought together in such a way that we can have our ambition and exercise humility at the same time. Perhaps. But at the very least we should acknowledge the tension here, that what we have is a situation about which most thoughtful Christians would likely feel conflicted, pulled as they are in very different directions.

Disciplined Formation

Although formation happens whether we are aware of it or not, most of us rightly assume that formation of a particular kind or direction requires disciplined and sustained effort. If we desire to become an accomplished ballerina, baseball player, violinist, or painter, we don't just sit around and hope we will one day wake up and it will be so. Rather, we know nothing short of years of disciplined and dedicated effort will be necessary if we are to have any hope of being so transformed. Similarly, year in and year out, parents make decisions about the formation of their children with the clear recognition that formation in a particular direction is not a matter of magic, but of disciplined and thoughtful action.

Why is it that all of us know being an athlete or artist requires discipline, but many of us too often assume being a follower of Jesus requires little or none? None of us would be so naïve as to believe we would simply wake up one day and be capable of playing the piano, yet many of us act as if the Christian life can be lived well without a similar intentionality.

For some of us this attitude stems, at least in part, from fear that the Christian faith will be transformed into a form of *works-righteousness*, by which we mean an attempt to earn God's favor through our actions. Of course we are right to insist, as does scripture, that our salvation is the result not of our works but of God's gracious initiative in and through Jesus Christ (Ephesians 2:8-9). Yet such an affirmation of God's grace should not be taken to mean that our *response* to that grace is insignificant, for as Paul goes on to tell the Ephesians: "For we are what [God] has made us, created in Christ Jesus for good works, which God prepared beforehand to be our way of life" (Ephesians 2:10). Christian formation is not, therefore, to be understood as an attempt to transform ourselves into super-Christians who can earn God's favor through good works; rather, Christian formation involves the slow process of being shaped by God's Spirit to daily present our entire lives to God as a "living sacrifice" in worshipful response to God's gracious initiative.

Of course, such living sacrifices are never offered in a cultural vacuum. This is why Christians must also pay careful attention to the cultures of formation within which they dwell.

The Power of Expectations

Whatever else cultures are, they are complex formation systems that shape us with certain expectations. To be at home in a particular culture is to know what to expect. For example, if you find yourself at home in the world of social media, it is because you have been formed in such a way that you have clear expectations about what kinds of things routinely happen there. As a result, you know what is expected of you and what you can expect of others in that particular setting.

The same could be said, of course, with respect to other spheres. College professors often find, for example, that students have very specific expectations about what will happen during the first class session of a new term. They expect the professor to walk into class, introduce herself, welcome them, read the roll, distribute and discuss the syllabus, give them their first assignment, and dismiss them early. (This last expectation is the strongest!)

Where and how did these students learn these expectations? The students didn't come out of the womb with these expectations, nor did they ever take a course entitled, "What to Expect on the First Day of Class." What they *did* do, however, was thoroughly (and largely unconsciously) internalize a whole set of experiences such that certain kinds of behavior, certain ways of doing things, came to be seen as normal and therefore expected.

Of course, social media and college classrooms are not the only kind of subcultures with their own sets of expectations and definitions of *normal*. We also speak about "corporate cultures" and "workplace cultures," which are every bit as formative for the way we see and experience our daily lives as any others. In these settings, certain behaviors and attitudes are considered normal and are therefore instilled largely through day-to-day participation in that culture.

If you have any doubts about the power of cultures to form expectations (and thus affect your comfort level), try to remember the last time you found yourself in a culture where you were *not* at home. Perhaps you traveled to a different country or even stepped into an unfamiliar subculture closer to home. What was it that made you feel out of place or not at home? For some, it might have been a different language, a different diet, or a different way of performing a routine activity (such as driving on the wrong side of the road). For others, it may have been some other clearly noticeable difference that made them less than fully comfortable.

Regardless of the specific differences, what often makes us most uneasy about a less-than familiar culture is the anxiety that accompanies not knowing what to expect. This anxiety is real whether you are stepping off the plane in another country, walking into an office on the first day of a new job, or slipping into the back row on your first Sunday at a new church. It's hard to relax if you're unsure about what is expected of you and what to expect of other people around you. It can be profoundly unsettling to always be wondering if something we are doing (or not doing) is unintentionally offending the sensibilities of those around us.

But cultural expectations do not merely affect our comfort level; they also influence the very way we see and interpret what's going on around us. Many first-century Jews, for example, had fairly specific expectations regarding God's promised and long-awaited Messiah. Thus, while some believed Jesus was indeed the Messiah, others had deep misgivings rooted in their expectations of what the Messiah ought to look like. Thus, when Philip tells Nathaniel they have "found him about whom Moses in the law and also the prophets wrote, Jesus son of Joseph from Nazareth," Nathaniel replies: "Can anything good come out of Nazareth?" (John 1:45-46). In other words, Nathaniel's expectations about Messiah (and Nazareth) made it difficult for him to see Jesus as the Messiah. In a similar way, Peter's understanding of the Messiah made it difficult for him to hear and accept Jesus's teaching about his impending suffering and death (Matthew 16:21-23).

Each of us likewise interprets and evaluates countless experiences in our everyday lives based primarily on the ways we have been shaped to understand the world around us. Just as people evaluated Jesus's messianic claim based on how they had been formed to understand what it meant to *be* Messiah, so we inevitably find ourselves evaluating such things as our marriages, our jobs, and our churches based on how we've been formed to think about their purposes. If we've been formed all our lives, for example, to believe marriage is primarily a means to personal happiness, then it will make perfectly good sense for us to evaluate our marriages on whether they are making us happy. In fact, our daily experience of marriage will likely be inseparable from our ongoing assessment of whether it is indeed furthering our happiness.

Now what does any of this have to do with Christian formation? Quite a lot. As Christians who are called to be *conformed* to the image of Christ, we ought to have a keen interest in the ways our lives and the lives of those around us are being formed. In short, we need to pay attention to the shape of our lives.

All of us are constantly being formed by the cultures of which we are a part; *formation happens.* The question is never simply *whether* we are being formed; we most certainly are. Rather, the more important question is always this: *Into what* are we being formed?

As noted above, every culture forms its citizens to see the world and act within it in certain ways that are regarded as normal within that culture. This process of formation is certainly complex, but we can begin to understand it better by paying attention to some of its most important parts. Every culture nourishes a certain way of life, a certain way of looking at and living in the world. This way of life has several interlocking elements including:

1. A set of *desires* or *longings.* What do we want out of life? What should we most desire?

2. A set of *convictions* or *core beliefs* regarding such things as the purpose of life, how the world works and one's place within it, and the proper means for evaluating success or failure in life.

3. A set of *dispositions* or *inclinations* to act in certain ways that, taken together, we call *character.*

Furthermore, every culture nourishes and instills these desires, convictions, and dispositions by several means, including the following:

4. Telling certain *stories*.

5. Engaging in certain *practices*.

6. Building and sustaining certain *institutions*.

The next six chapters in this book will take up each one of these central aspects of formation. Because these six elements are closely intertwined, we could reasonably begin with any one of them. Thus, the order in which these six elements are taken up should not be viewed as a commentary on their relative importance but merely as an admission that it's difficult to try to talk about six things at once!

As you proceed through this book and are asked to think hard about and pay attention to matters that often escape our attention, always keep in mind the central reason for undertaking this exploration: as followers of Jesus Christ, we are called to have our lives formed and animated by the Spirit of Jesus. Yet how shall we discern whether or to what extent this is indeed happening? One way to put ourselves in a better position to make such discernments is to explore how human beings come to be formed and animated. Once we better understand how we are being formed and animated in our everyday lives, we may be in a better position to ask more pointed questions about who or what is predominantly influencing the overall shape of our lives.

Questions for Personal Reflection and Group Discussion

1. As you think about your life, what people, events, and experiences have been the most formative for you? Take one or two of these major formative influences and carefully reflect on how specifically you came to be formed through them.

2. Has there been a time in your life when you were intensely aware you were being formed? If so, what were the circumstances and what contributed to this awareness? If not, in what ways were you being formed that you were not aware of?

3. As you think about your family members, friends, co-workers, and your neighbors, what would you identify as the most formative influences on their lives? What basis do you have for thinking so?

4. What are some of the most obvious ways your congregation or parish functions as a community of formation? In other words, where do you see formation taking place among your people on a regular basis? Where else might it also be taking place in less obvious ways?

Two

Desires

O God, you are my God, I seek you,
my soul thirsts for you;
my flesh faints for you,
as in a dry and weary land
where there is no water.
–Psalm 63:1-2

I am the Alpha and the Omega, the beginning
and the end. To the thirsty I will give water as a
gift from the spring of the water of life.
–Revelation 21:6b

You have made us for yourself, O Lord,
and our hearts are restless until they find their
rest in you.
–St. Augustine

Revealing Desires

Some psychologists have suggested that one of the primary animating forces in our lives is *desire*. Indeed, if there's some truth to the old adage "We are what we eat," then there's also likely some truth to the notion that "We are what we want." Who we are and who we become are intimately connected to our past, present, and future desires.

What is it that you care most deeply about? What are your deepest desires, dreams, and aspirations? What is the desired future you strive to live into? Whether we are conscious of it or not, these desires have an enormous impact on the shape and experience of our everyday lives. It takes only a moment's reflection to realize that a particular way of life is shaped not only by a person's past, but also by a particular desired and imagined future. In other words, just as our pasts are never simply past (because that past still shapes and influences our present life), so the future we imagine is never simply future (because much of our present energy is expended seeking to live into that imagined future.)

What are these desires and where do they come from? Not surprisingly, not everyone agrees about this. Some psychologists believe we are born with certain basic needs and the desire to meet them. These needs may be physiological (air, food, sleep), psychological (stability, security) or social (to belong and be loved). Others argue that even if we have these basic needs, the specific ways we learn to recognize them as needs and meet them are just that—learned. Still others have argued that all our desires and longings—whatever they are—are simply pointers to the *one* desire that God created at the center of every person: the desire to be in communion with God. It was this desire Augustine addressed when he spoke of our restless hearts.

It is important to note that Christian teaching is *not* that human desire is evil and therefore to be extinguished. Indeed, according to the Christian faith, our problem as humans is not that our lives are animated by longing, but that our lives are so often driven by the *wrong* desires. For example, the seven deadly sins illustrate our inclination to destructive desires. As a result, the Christian life is about being formed to want the right things in the right ways for the right reasons. To repeat: Christians are not those who lack or suppress all desire, but those who (by God's grace) are learning to desire rightly.

So how does this process of learning work?

Our Desires and God's Desires

Perhaps one place to start is with the frank acknowledgement that what we have been formed to desire for ourselves and what God

37

desires for us are often quite different. To paraphrase God's insistence in Isaiah 55:8: "My desires are not your desires, nor my longings your longings." This is not least because we live in a society that forms us to pursue relentlessly our own desires, our own happiness. Interestingly enough, in the United States we even have a name for a particular set of longings and desires that we are all encouraged to pursue: We call it "the American Dream." But followers of Jesus know life isn't simply about pursuing their own happiness or even the happiness of their children or family members. Indeed, those who seek to follow the way of Jesus know life is not first of all about doing what we desire, but about doing what God desires. More to the point, followers of Jesus seek to be so transformed that one day their own desires will be aligned with God's desires. Just as Jesus's prayer in the Garden of Gethsemane— "not my will but yours be done" (Luke 22:42)—was characteristic of his entire life, so we seek to be animated by God's desires for us and for God's world. This, after all, is surely part of what we ask in praying the Lord's Prayer: "Your kingdom come, Your will be done, on earth as it is in heaven," (Matthew 6:10).

We pray and work for the day when God's desires are as fully enacted in our lives and throughout all of God's creation as they are in that realm we call heaven.

What are God's desires? Obviously, there's no short answer to this question. But just as we sometimes use the phrase "the American Dream" as shorthand for that vision of a particular future many devote their entire lives to pursuing (and sustaining), so the gospels speak of the "kingdom of God" or the "reign of God" as that social order toward which God is moving all of creation and to which God's people offer themselves in service.

What desires animate that kingdom? We glimpse part of an answer in Luke 15, where Jesus is faced with the grumbling of the scribes and Pharisees who were offended that he was welcoming and eating with tax collectors and other notorious sinners. In response, Jesus tells three parables (the lost sheep, the lost coin, and the lost sons), each of which in its own way underscores a central truth of the gospel: God has an unquenchable desire for *us*, a desire that leads God to pursue us relentlessly and to rejoice when we are found. The shepherd leaves behind the other sheep and goes looking for the one lost sheep; the woman searches diligently for her one lost coin until she finds it; and the father, seeing his returning son in the distance, violates all social propriety and runs rejoicing to embrace him.

Thus, whatever we might say about the desires Christians have or ought to have, such statements should always be framed by the recognition that just as "we love because [God] first loved us" (1 John 4:19), so also we desire and pursue

God because God first desires and pursues us. And as the apostle Paul declares in Romans 8:38-39, there's no reason to believe God's desires will be easily thwarted:

> For I am convinced that neither death, nor life, nor angels, nor rulers, nor things present, nor things to come, nor powers, nor height, nor depth, nor anything else in all creation, will be able to separate us from the love of God in Christ Jesus our Lord.

It is vital that we all pay greater attention to the potential conflict between the desires our culture teaches us to pursue and the desires God wishes for us. At the very least, formation entails both paying close attention to the desires that currently animate our daily lives and being open to cultivating a different set of desires that will be at the center of our lives.

Schooling Our Wants

One helpful way we might summarize all this is by considering how human desire is educated—that is, how our varied wants and longings are not untainted, uninfluenced private wishes but are, instead, expressions of our being schooled over time in particular kinds of formative environments: family life, say, or popular culture, or social media. If, for instance, the advertising industry instructs us in what kind of car we should want or what constitutes a good life, thoughtful Christians will need to be alert to the ways such an education of desire is at odds with the call to a different kind of life and a different set of desires. We will need to regularly remind ourselves and each other that life in the body of Christ is its own school of counter-formation for those who seek to have their desires educated differently. This call to a different life, a life marked by a different set of desires, is expressed clearly in 1 Peter 1:13-16:

> Therefore prepare your minds for action; discipline yourselves; set all your hope on the grace that Jesus Christ will bring you when he is revealed. Like obedient children, do not be conformed to the desires that you formerly had in ignorance. Instead, as he who called you is holy, be holy yourselves in all your conduct; for it is written, "You shall be holy, for I am holy."

Questions for Personal Reflection and Group Discussion

1. What are one or two desires or longings that most clearly shape your daily life? How did they come to play such a central role in your life?

2. If you were to identify one or two desires you wish had a greater impact on the shape of your daily life, what would they be? How might your

day-to-day be different if these desires exerted a greater force?

3. Where in your life do you most feel the tension or conflict of competing desires? In other words, where are one or two places in your life where different longings seem to be at odds (if not at war) with each other, resulting in your being pulled in very different (if not opposite) directions?

4. Consider the three questions above, but instead of answering as an individual, think about your parish or congregation. How do specific desires and longings affect the formation of your community?

Three

Convictions

O Most High, when I am afraid,
I put my trust in you.
In God, whose word I praise,
in God I trust; I am not afraid;
what can flesh do to me?
–Psalm 56:2b-4

But if we have died with Christ, we believe that
we will also live with him. We know that Christ,
being raised from the dead, will never die again;
death no longer has dominion over him. The
death he died, he died to sin, once for all; but the
life he lives, he lives to God. So you also must
consider yourselves dead to sin and alive to God
in Christ Jesus."
–Romans 6:8-11

"This I Believe"

In the early 1950s, celebrated journalist Edward R. Murrow produced and hosted a popular radio program entitled, "This I Believe." The purpose of the program was to allow citizens from all walks of life an opportunity to articulate the fundamental convictions or core beliefs that guided their everyday lives. In the spring of 2005, a new series of "This I Believe" essays were broadcast on public radio stations across the United States. Although neither program presumed to tell listeners what they should believe, both programs rightly assumed that if we are to understand what animates the lives of our neighbors, then we will need to understand their fundamental beliefs or convictions.

Convictions are those deeply held beliefs that shape and inform our everyday experience of the world. How do convictions do this? In short, the convictions we have about the world suggest both how we ought to live in it *and* how to evaluate our current life within it. To get a feel for how this works, ask yourself the following questions:

- Do you believe human life has a purpose? If so, what would you say it is?

- What does it mean to live a good life? In other words, what kinds of things are necessary for human well-being and flourishing? What does a person fundamentally need to live well?

- Do you believe human beings have a basic nature? If so, how would you characterize it?

- Do you believe people can change?

- Do you think people generally get what they deserve, or do you tend to think life is basically unfair?

- Who or what is worthy of your complete trust?

Although the answers to none of these questions are simple or straightforward, we all likely have rather well-defined convictions about each one. But where did these deeply held beliefs come from? Again, none of us came out of the womb believing what we do about these and countless other matters. None of us likely took a class that gave us the answers to any of these questions. Indeed, odds are most of us give very little direct attention to any of these matters on a regular basis.

Yet it would be a huge mistake to assume that such fundamental convictions—and others like them—don't affect the shape and direction of our everyday lives.

The Strength of our Convictions

Every culture encourages us to believe some things rather than others about these and other fundamental questions. Such convictions are central to our identity because they represent part of the reservoir we draw from in our daily lives. For example, do you believe all or most poor people are lazy and are therefore largely responsible for their own plight? If so, you will have certain ideas about if or how to help them. Do you believe most strangers will hurt you if given the opportunity? If so, this conviction will shape your understanding of what it means to engage in the biblical practice of hospitality. Do you believe war and violence are sometimes the only possible responses to evil? If so, this will likely shape the way you hear Jesus's call to love our enemies and his call to pray for those who persecute us. In short, our convictions go a long way toward shaping our imaginations regarding the kind of world we live in and what it means to live and act in that world. Thus, the beliefs we hold are not mere mental operations or private opinions; our convictions exert a profound influence on how we understand the world around us and how we behave in it.

Our convictions form us to see a particular world (one that is inherently unjust, for instance). Because we act in the world we see, asking hard questions about such beliefs (and where they come from) is crucial to those who desire to be conformed to the image of Christ.

We will shortly take up the issue of *how* these convictions are formed within us, but first we need to become more aware of the central role that convictions play in our experience and assessment of everyday life. One way to deepen this awareness is to pay attention to the convictions that inform our lives and the lives of those around us, because the ways people think, feel, and act are nearly always closely related to their deepest convictions. For example, imagine you have an acquaintance named Tom who believes human life is basically a race to the top. For Tom, the whole point of human existence is to excel in one's chosen field and climb as high and as quickly as possible up that field's ladder of success. Not surprisingly, this fundamental conviction will inevitably guide many of Tom's decisions and actions in (and beyond) the workplace. It's likely, for instance, Tom will view fellow co-workers primarily as competitors for scarce resources such as promotions, raises, and titles. As a result, Tom will be less inclined to work cooperatively with others, because aiding another's advancement might impede his own. Tom might also be inclined to view home life primarily as a personal support system that enables and facilitates his race to the top. To the extent that it functions well in this respect, Tom may feel good about his home life. Should his family, however, unduly complicate or hamper his progress, he may find himself frustrated and dissatisfied with family life.

It's also likely Tom will find himself evaluating other arenas of his life in similar ways. He may, for example, come to evaluate his experience of the church largely based on how well it supports his chosen life goals. If it facilitates those goals, or perhaps even helps him cope with the fallout from their pursuit, then he may find himself evaluating his church experience positively. If, however, the church ever begins to question the fundamental appropriateness of those life goals, Tom may find himself irritated by what he perceives as the church's meddling in his personal affairs.

Of course it's not simply Tom's experience of work, home, or church life that comes to be evaluated in terms of his guiding conviction about the point or purpose of life. Tom's overall sense of how a particular day or week went, or even how his life in general is going, will inevitably be tied to his sense of how much progress he is making up the ladder of success.

The point of this very simple example is to provide a glimpse of how a single guiding conviction impacts the shape and experience of one's life. The way we think, the way we act, the way we feel—all have direct ties to the deep convictions we hold. The reality of our everyday lives is, of course, much more complex than the above example, not least because our lives are usually guided by a number of different (and sometimes competing or conflicting) convictions. Yet the example can nevertheless encourage us to examine our core beliefs, the fundamental convictions that guide our everyday decisions.

If you were asked to sit down right now and write an essay for the "This I Believe" series that would articulate your core convictions and thereby make sense of the shape of your current life, what would you write? What, in other words, would someone need to know about your deepest convictions to make sense of the way you live? Or perhaps even more to the point, what might others surmise as your deepest convictions by looking at the shape of your current life?

A Matter of Trust

If you were to write such an essay, it's very likely that one of the primary matters you would address is where you place your trust, for trust is one of the most fundamental orienting factors in human life. Although we're not always aware of it consciously, we place our trust in something or someone all the time, and this posture of trust goes a long way toward defining the shape of our lives. To put this differently: The shape of our lives is influenced not only by what we believe *about* the world, but also by what or who we believe *in*. It's one thing, for example, to believe (intellectually) that your coworker is trustworthy; it's another to believe in that coworker enough to trust her to babysit your children or to communicate with your most lucrative client.

It may be worth noting at this point that the biblical notion of faith involves not simply believing that something is the case, but also believing in some*one*. As the author of the book of James suggests, even the demons are orthodox (in the sense of holding right beliefs), for even they believe God is one (2:19). Presumably, the difference between the demons and those of us who seek to follow Jesus is not primarily a matter of what we believe about God; rather, the difference is more fundamentally a matter of whether we trust in God and the ways of God. The demons refuse to place their trust in God and the ways of God, while followers of Jesus are called, with the empowerment of the Holy Spirit, to do precisely that.

In his letter to the Romans, the apostle Paul explained the centrality of faith and trust to the Christian life by appealing to the example of Abraham, our father in the faith:

> Hoping against hope, he believed that he would become "the father of many nations," according to what was said, "So numerous shall your descendants be." He did not weaken in faith when he considered his own body, which was already as good as dead (for he was about a hundred years old), or when

he considered the barrenness of Sarah's womb. No distrust made him waver concerning the promise of God, but he grew strong in his faith as he gave glory to God, being fully convinced that God was able to do what he had promised. (Romans 4:18-21)

Abraham trusted God because he was convinced God was able to do what God had promised. Yet like all of us, Abraham was not as steadfast as the God who called him, and so Abraham sometimes trusted his own ways more than the ways of God. (See Genesis 16 for one obvious example.) Nevertheless, we—like Abraham—are called to place our trust in God and the ways of God. Indeed, such trust, such faith, is to be the fundamental posture of our entire lives.

But is it? If we are honest with ourselves about our everyday lives, in what or whom do we actually place our trust? More than likely, over the course of a day or week, most of us place (and are encouraged to place) varying degrees of trust in quite a number of different things: our family members; our neighbors and co-workers; strangers in the car next to us speeding down the highway; the laws of the land and our system of government; our police and military forces; our physical senses; the general orderliness of the universe; our reason and education; our experience and instincts; and our own abilities and hard work—just to name a few. That's a lot of trust, and not all of it is misplaced, because it's difficult to imagine any life that didn't trust some of these things at least some of the time. Even so, we would be wise to explore just how easy it is to place too much trust in everyday things. As alluded to earlier, the advertising industry often uses imagery that exploits this tendency. Will a particular food create idyllic family meal times? Will this new car infuse my life with adventure? Such misplaced trust is often at the heart of what scripture means by idolatry. Yet most of us probably know—at least intellectually—that we are called to place our ultimate trust in the God of Jesus Christ. So here's the real question: In light of all these things we routinely place our trust in, what would it mean—and just as importantly, what might it *look like*—for us to say, with the psalmist, that we place our trust in God?

The Way that Leads to Life

Certainly, no brief study can do justice to what it means to place our trust fully in God. Yet perhaps a couple of central issues can be raised in ways that will place this crucial matter at the center of the church's agenda once again and offer thoughtful Christians plenty to think about and discuss together.

Most of us would acknowledge that trusting God means placing our very lives in God's hands. Yet what does that look like in daily life? At a minimum, it requires us to trust that there is more to life than we can see with our human eyes. It requires us to trust that in the person of Jesus we really do come face to face with God and the ways of God. It requires us to trust that the ways of God really do lead to life. This fundamental posture of trust is rooted in one of the most central convictions of the church: that in Jesus Christ we see most clearly who God is. But the church has *also* always insisted that in Jesus Christ we see most clearly who *we* are called to be, for in Christ we receive not only the most complete image available of what God is like, but also the most complete image available of what it means to be fully human. God's call to be conformed to the image of Christ, therefore, is a call to life, a call to live life as it was created to be lived.

But walking in the way of Jesus—a way that is grounded in mercy, compassion and forgiveness—will require us to trust in the ways of God, because the world's wide and well-worn paths too often lead in an entirely different direction. The world forms us to believe the way of Jesus is impractical, utopian, and unrealistic. In contrast, followers of Jesus live their lives based on the conviction that the way of Jesus is not simply how God deals with us, but also the way God desires us to deal with others. In short, as Christians we are called to trust fully that human life is never more beautiful than when it is lived in conformity to the way of Jesus. Such a life is one not only marked by integrity and wholeness, but one which is dedicated to being an *agent* of healing and wholeness in the world—a vessel through which the love and mercy of God freely flows.

As we all know all too well, there are many obstacles to living such a life. We live in a culture increasingly animated less by trust than by fear. As inhabitants of this fearful culture, we find ourselves torn almost daily between the call to trust God and God's ways and the temptation to be driven by our own fears, real and imagined. Throughout our lifetimes, all of us face fears of different kinds: of failure, of rejection, of injury and illness, and ultimately, of death itself. But a life lived in the grip of fear has little hope of being a beautiful life. The good news of the gospel, however, is that in Jesus Christ we are freed from the stranglehold fear—including the fear of death—has on our lives. In Jesus Christ we are freed to live an abundant life, grounded in a fundamental trust of God and God's ways. For as Paul poignantly asked his brothers and sisters in Rome, "If God is for us, who can be against us?" (Romans 8:31).

As followers of Jesus, we are called to live out together our conviction that the God revealed in Jesus Christ is worthy of our ultimate trust and allegiance. Doing so will no doubt call us to hold other fundamental convictions about the world and our place within it. What are some of these other fundamental convictions, and in what ways are they similar to and different from the convictions other people hold? And how exactly are Christians in their everyday lives to live out these convictions?

These are all important questions; indeed, the point of this field guide is to encourage conversations that might help us begin formulating thoughtful responses to such crucial matters. Are there easy answers to these questions? Probably not. But there's good reason to believe that in discussing them seriously with one another, we might begin to see more clearly both the shape of our current lives and the shape of the life to which God has called us.

Food for Thought

In the newer "This I Believe" series, journalist Sara Miles spoke of how her understanding of belief changed when she—an avowed skeptic—received communion for the first time. In her own words:

I came to believe that God is revealed not only in bread and wine during church services, but whenever we share food with others — particularly strangers. I came to believe that the fruits of creation are for everyone, without exception — not something to be doled out to insiders or the "deserving."

So, over the objections of some of my fellow parishioners, I started a food pantry right in the church sanctuary, giving away literally tons of oranges and potatoes and Cheerios around the very same altar where I'd eaten the body of Christ. We gave food to anyone who showed up. I met thieves, child abusers, millionaires, day laborers, politicians, schizophrenics, gangsters, bishops — all blown into my life through the restless power of a call to feed people.

At the pantry, serving over 500 strangers a week, I confronted the same issues that had kept me from religion in the first place. Like church, the food pantry asked me to leave certainty behind, tangled me up with people I didn't particularly want to know and scared me with its demand for more faith than I was ready to give.

Because my new vocation didn't turn out to be as simple as going to church on Sundays and declaring myself "saved." I had to trudge in the rain through housing projects, sit on the curb wiping the runny nose of a psychotic man, take the firing pin out of a battered woman's Magnum and then stick the gun in a cookie tin in the trunk of my car. I had to struggle with my atheist family, my doubting friends, and the prejudices and traditions of my newfound church.

But I learned that hunger can lead to more life — that by sharing real food, I'd find communion with the most unlikely people; that by eating a piece of bread, I'd experience myself as part of one body. This I believe: that by opening ourselves to strangers, we will taste God.[2]

Questions for Personal Reflection and Group Discussion

1. Identify one or two fundamental convictions or core beliefs that clearly shape your daily life. (If you need help getting started, you may want to refer back to the list at the beginning of this chapter.) In what specific ways do these convictions influence the shape of your life? How did these come to play such a central role in your life?

2. Are there one or two convictions you wish had a *greater impact* on the shape of your daily life? How do you imagine your life would be different if they *did* have a greater formative influence? How do you account for the relative lack of influence these convictions have on the shape of your life currently?

3. Consider the two questions above, but instead of answering as an individual, think about your parish or congregation. How do convictions and

[2] Miles, S. (2008, May 5). *Strangers Bring Us Closer to God.* NPR.
https://www.npr.org/2008/05/05/90133974/strangers-bring-us-closer-to-god

core beliefs influence the formation of your community?

4. Reflect further on your community of faith. Who comes to mind when you think of people whose everyday lives are marked by a fundamental posture of trust in God and the ways of God? What is it about the shape of these people's lives that suggests they trust God deeply? What insights do you then have about your own life and relationship with God?

Four

Character

The LORD is merciful and gracious, slow to anger and abounding in steadfast love. He will not always accuse, nor will he keep his anger forever. He does not deal with us according to our sins, nor repay us according to our iniquities. For as the heavens are high above the earth, so great is his steadfast love toward those who fear him; as far as the east is from the west, so far he removes our transgressions from us. As a father has compassion for his children, so the LORD has compassion for those who fear him.
–Psalm 103:8-13

As God's chosen ones, holy and beloved, clothe yourselves with compassion, kindness, humility,

meekness, and patience. Bear with one another and, if anyone has a complaint against another, forgive each other; just as the Lord has forgiven you, so you also must forgive. Above all, clothe yourselves with love, which binds everything together in perfect harmony. And let the peace of Christ rule in your hearts, to which indeed you were called in the one body. And be thankful.
—Colossians 3:12-15

The Character of Our Lives

Every culture forms its inhabitants to be inclined to act in certain ways. How are you inclined to act, for example, sitting at a stoplight when the only car in front of you hasn't moved an inch five seconds after the light has turned green? How are you disposed to respond at a party when someone insults you or cuts you down? Or how are you likely to respond when you get word that one of your personal enemies—someone who has gone out of his or her way to make your life miserable—suddenly has a bit of misfortune themselves?

To say all of us have been formed in ways that incline us toward certain responses in such situations is not to excuse our responses. Rather, it is to acknowledge the dynamics of human behavior are often more complicated than they first appear. Up to this point, we have noted that people are animated both by certain *desires* and by certain *convictions* they hold about the world and their place within it. We now turn to look briefly at another dimension of our shape, an aspect that is both formed by those around us and serves as another animating force in our lives. This dimension we call *character*.

The language of character points to something important (yet elusive) about the dynamics of human behavior: Human behavior is neither completely predictable nor completely random. Rather, over time people's lives show certain patterns and take on certain shapes such that we feel justified in making judgments about the kind of people they are. The distinctive shape of a human life made visible through behavior patterns is what we mean by *character*. We see our neighbor battle cancer over many months with an indomitable spirit, and we feel justified in calling her courageous and brave. We work for years for an employer who consistently looks out for the well-being of his employees, and we feel justified in saying he is just and fair. Over the years we watch a mother care for her young child with disabilities, striving to help him cope with the basics of life, and we feel justified in calling her patient and steadfast.

Does this mean our neighbor has never acted cowardly, or our employer has never acted unjustly, or this mother has never lost her patience with her little boy? Of course not. Rather, it means we have seen enough of this person's life to feel confident about the ways in which they are typically inclined or disposed to act. Can we ever predict for sure how they or anyone else will act in a particular situation? No, but we still think it possible to name certain commendable patterns we see in people's lives, patterns we identify as courage, justice, and patience. These qualities allow us not so much to predict another person's behavior as much as they enable us to point to behavior we think worthy of imitation.

In short, over time each of us is formed in such a way as to be inclined or disposed to act in certain ways rather than others. When these inclinations and dispositions result in patterns of behavior that are commendable and worthy of imitation we name them as virtues; when they result in patterns of behavior to be avoided, we name them as vices. The distinctive shape of a life resulting from all of this taken together is what we mean by character.

But how do we determine the kinds of behavior worth imitating? How do we determine which virtues are to be nurtured and which vices avoided? To answer that question, we need to explore a bit further the notion of virtue.

The Excellence of Christ

For many of us, virtue language has been all but ruined, conjuring up images of prudes and other killjoys promoting a rigid set of rules. If this is what it means to be virtuous, we think, then many of us want nothing to do with it. But the concept of virtue is much broader (and much more interesting!) than this. In fact, whether we ever use the word or not, the concept of virtue is woven deeply into the fabric of any society or culture.

What is a virtue? At its most basic level, a virtue is simply a form of excellence. For example, the virtues of a championship racehorse are its strength, speed, and stamina, while the virtue of a wristwatch is its accuracy in keeping time. Similarly, we are frequently told that ketchup ought to be thick and apps on our phones ought to be user-friendly. These examples illustrate two important observations. First, the virtue or excellence of something is always tied directly to its purpose. In other words, if you're convinced the purpose of a watch is to keep accurate time, you'll have a ready basis on which to make judgments about whether this or that watch displays this excellence or virtue. And second, if the four examples listed above seem straightforward, it is due to relatively widespread agreements about the purposes of racehorses, watches, ketchups, and apps.

Thus, even though nearly everything around us can (and is) evaluated according to some standard of excellence (or virtue), the more people disagree about the purpose of something, the more people will disagree about what will count for excellence. What are the virtues of a good restaurant? That will depend upon your convictions regarding the primary purposes of restaurants. What makes a good elementary school? That will depend upon what you think schools are for. In a similar way, when people make judgments about the virtues of a particular congregation or parish, they reveal—whether they recognize it or not—their convictions about the purpose of the church. Not surprisingly, if people disagree about the fundamental purposes of restaurants, schools or churches they will also likely disagree about what makes a good or excellent one.

As you might imagine, matters are no less complicated when we turn to human beings. What virtues or excellences should humans embody? How should human beings be disposed to act in certain situations? To answer these questions is already to reveal one's convictions about the fundamental purposes of human life. In short, any list of virtues or human excellences (and vices) reveals what people believe the shape of life ought (or ought not) to look like. Thus, when public schools seek through character education programs to instill in students certain civic virtues (such as civility, open-mindedness, and respect for authority), they reveal something about the kind of people they believe are necessary for a democratic society to function well. In a similar way, employers who seek to instill in their employees workplace virtues such as reliability, loyalty, and efficiency do so because people with such virtues will help that enterprise be successful.

To ask about the virtues or the patterns of behavior that ought to be at the heart of the Christian life is likewise to inquire about the desired shape of human life. Here, however, the goal is not primarily a responsible citizen or a productive employee, but a child of God conformed to the image of Jesus Christ. In other words, the virtues or excellences Christians are called to live out are the excellences they see revealed in the One who lived human life as it was intended—Jesus Christ. The church is therefore called, for example, to be a community of compassion as a witness to the compassionate God revealed first to Israel and then most perfectly in and through Jesus Christ. Our character, in short, ought to reflect something of the character of God.

As Christians, we do not believe we can live such lives of virtue or excellence apart from God's grace and the working of God's Spirit. Nevertheless, we do believe God can transform the shape of our lives and the patterns of our behavior to bring them more into conformity to the pattern we see in Jesus Christ. After all, if we claim we are followers of Jesus, and if we insist the Spirit of Christ is working in and through us, shouldn't we expect that over time some transformation would take place? The apostle Paul was convinced the Spirit is transforming us into the image of Christ:

> And all of us, with unveiled faces, seeing the glory of the Lord as though reflected in a mirror, are being transformed into the same image from one degree of glory to another; for this comes from the Lord, the Spirit. (2 Corinthians 3:18)

Paul was very clear that this transformation was not merely an invisible transformation; rather, it involved bearing real behavioral fruit, fruit that was the natural outcome of the Spirit's work in our lives: "...the fruit of the Spirit is love, joy, peace, patience, kindness, generosity, faithfulness, gentleness, and self-control," (Galatians 5:22-23).

So learning to pay attention to the fruit (the virtues or vices) being nurtured in our lives is not for the purpose of encouraging pride (or despair) but so we might cultivate the kind of alert, honest reckoning necessary for the life of discipleship. How will we know if the Spirit is bearing good fruit in our lives if we're afraid to look and see what fruit is actually growing there? Moreover, the church also pays attention to the character of its community because that life is a potentially eloquent witness to the power of God's Spirit to transform. As Jesus suggests in the passage from the Sermon on the Mount quoted above, we are called to be salt and light not for our own sake, but for the sake of those around us, so that in seeing our good works others may give glory to God.

This is why Paul could boldly encourage others to "Be imitators of me, as I am of Christ," (1 Corinthians 11:1). Paul did not believe the Christian life consisted only in believing certain things about Jesus Christ, but also in the willingness to be transformed by God's grace into the people we were created to be. This willingness required that Paul's listeners set their minds on certain things and to keep on *doing* certain things as well. May we take his words of admonition to heart as well:

> Finally, beloved, whatever is true, whatever is honorable, whatever is just, whatever is pure, whatever is pleasing, whatever is commendable, if there is any excellence and if there is anything worthy of praise, think about these things. Keep on doing the things that you have learned and received and heard and seen in me, and the God of peace will be with you. (Philippians 4:8-9)

A Study in Character

In his book, *War is a Force that Gives Us Meaning*, journalist Chris Hedges tells the story of meeting the Soraks, a Bosnian Serb couple in a largely Muslim enclave of Goražde. The couple were indifferent to the nationalist propaganda of the

Bosnian Serb leadership. But when the Serbs started to bomb their town, the Muslim leadership in the community became hostile to them, and eventually the Soraks lost their two sons to Muslim forces. One of their sons was a few months shy of becoming a father. In the city under siege, conditions got worse and worse, and in the midst of this, Rosa Sorak's widowed daughter-in-law gave birth to a baby girl. With food shortages, the elderly and infants were dying in droves, and after a short time, the baby, given only tea to drink, began to fade. Meanwhile, on the eastern edge of Goražde, Fadil Fejzić, an illiterate Muslim farmer, kept his cow, milking her by night so as to avoid Serbian snipers. On the fifth day of the baby having only tea, just before dawn, Fejzić appeared at the door with a half a liter of milk for the baby. He refused money. He came back with milk every day for 442 days, until the daughter-in-law and granddaughter left for Serbia. Other families in the street started to insult him, telling him to give his milk to Muslims and let the *četnik* (the pejorative term for Serbs) die. But he did not relent.

Later, the Soraks moved and lost touch with Fejzić, but Hedges went and sought him out. The cow had been slaughtered for meat before the end of the siege, and Fejzić had fallen on hard times. But, as Hedges says, "When I told him I had seen the Soraks, his eyes brightened. 'And the baby?' he asked. 'How is she?'"

In this moving story, we see something of how character is embodied. The farmer had been formed over time in such a way that generosity and compassion were central to his identity—to his way of being and living in the world—so that even in the face of danger and persecution, he could do no other than to act generously and compassionately.

Questions for Personal Reflection and Group Discussion

1. As noted above, every list of virtues is rooted in certain convictions about what counts for a good life. Make a list of what you believe are the most important human virtues. Then, go back over your list and try to discern what it reveals about your convictions regarding human life and flourishing.

2. Next, make a list of those virtues you see most often commended by the wider society through social media, advertising, popular culture, etc. What does this list reveal about what human life is presumably about?

3. What are two or three virtues most regularly displayed in your own life? Take one of these virtues and reflect on how it was formed within you. What about virtues you wish were displayed more regularly? What are the obstacles to the nurturing of these virtues?

4. Consider the above questions from the perspective of your community of faith, rather than as an individual. What virtues are or are not displayed in and through your parish or congregation? What contributed to this formation, and how might different virtues be more intentionally cultivated in the future?

Stories

The next day he saw Jesus coming towards him and declared, 'Here is the Lamb of God who takes away the sin of the world! This is he of whom I said, "After me comes a man who ranks ahead of me because he was before me." I myself did not know him; but I came baptizing with water for this reason, that he might be revealed to Israel.' And John testified, 'I saw the Spirit descending from heaven like a dove, and it remained on him. I myself did not know him, but the one who sent me to baptize with water said to me, "He on whom you see the Spirit descend and remain is the one who baptizes with the Holy Spirit." And I myself have seen and have testified that this is the Son of God.
¬John 1:29-34

That same day Jesus went out of the house and sat beside the lake. Such great crowds gathered around him that he got into a boat and sat there, while the whole crowd stood on the beach. And he told them many things in parables...
–Matthew 13:1-3a

Up to this point we have focused on the *what* of formation, that is, on *what* is being formed. Attending to the formation of our desires, convictions, and character is important because these have an enormous influence on the ways we experience and evaluate our everyday lives. In short, the shape of our lives is inseparable from the longings we have, the convictions we hold, and the character we embody. But it is also inseparable from the stories we tell, the practices we engage in, and the institutions which structure and support all the rest. Thus, our next several chapters will shift our focus to these three additional aspects of formation—stories, practices, and institutions—as a way of exploring the *how* of formation.

The Centrality of Stories

Stories are an incredibly important part of human life. We are, as some have noted, *story-shaped* creatures. Whether we recognize it consciously or not, we constantly seek to make sense of our lives and the lives of those around us through certain stories. For example, if you were given an hour or two to introduce yourself to a group of strangers, you would most likely not offer them a list of disconnected facts about yourself (date of birth, social security number, home address, etc.); rather, you would offer some version of your life story. You might recount for them certain pivotal events, significant relationships, and key experiences you believe offer insight into how you came to be where and who you are. Indeed, we often use phrases like "chapters of our lives," "turning the page," "an open book" or "closing the book" to describe elements of our life story.

Yet we understand ourselves not simply through the personal stories we tell about our own lives, but perhaps even more definitively through the larger, more comprehensive narratives that frame our personal stories. These larger narratives provide the socioeconomic, geographic, historical, and relational language with which we tell our personal stories. Many Jews, for example, have for millennia understood their identity as inseparable from the story of God's covenant with Abraham and of God's action in delivering Abraham's descendants from Egyptian bondage. Indeed, so closely is God— 'the LORD' (in Hebrew, YHWH; Exodus 3:14)—bound to this people that this God is repeatedly identified not as some remote, generic deity, but precisely as "the LORD your God, who brought you out of the land of Egypt" (Exodus 20:2; Leviticus 19:36; Numbers

15:41; Deuteronomy. 54 5:6). For many Jews today, therefore, this God, this event, and this people are bound together in ways that can only be understood by retelling and reliving this story.

Christians likewise come to understand who they are and who they are called to be in light of the story of "God-with-us" narrated in scripture and retold in and through the life of the church over the centuries. Like Jews, Christians understand themselves as creatures made in the image of God (Genesis 1:26-27) who have been given the responsibility of being faithful stewards of God's good creation. And just as Jews insist who they are is inseparable from God's promises to their ancestors and God's action in liberating them from Egyptian bondage, so Christians insist their own identity is inseparable from this same God's action in and through the life, death, and resurrection of Jesus of Nazareth and the ongoing work of God's Spirit.

Such claims may seem strange to those of us who are not accustomed to thinking of ourselves in terms of such large encompassing stories. Yet it may be that stories play a much larger role in the shape of our lives than we normally think. To begin to understand this, we need to step back and look more closely at how we use stories all the time to make sense of our world and our place in it.

The Character of Stories

Stories are a crucial aspect of our experience of human life not least because actions do not interpret themselves. That is, our actions—and the actions of others—only make sense when in some narrative framework or story. All of us have experienced this whenever we have been misunderstood because the story someone used to interpret our actions was very different from the story we told ourselves.

Imagine, for example, that Sue has been coming home late from work every night for a couple weeks. When her husband, Bob, asks her to try to be home for dinner the next evening, Sue promises to be on time. The next evening, however, Sue walks in the door an hour late. How are we to understand her actions? Clearly, "being an hour-later-than-promised for dinner" neither explains her actions nor gives us (or Bob) enough context to interpret or evaluate her tardiness. To explain why she was late, Sue would tell a story about what happened. We can, of course, imagine any number of possible stories Sue might tell, and how Bob evaluates Sue's tardiness will be bound up with the story she tells (and whether or not he believes her).

Presuming for the moment that Bob has every reason to believe Sue is telling the truth, notice how our evaluation of Sue changes depending on which of the following two stories she tells:

- "I'm sorry, Bob, for being late again. I guess I just got so caught up in the project I was working on that I totally lost track of time."

- "I'm sorry, Bob, for being late again. I really tried to be here on time; really, I did. In fact, I wanted to keep my promise so badly that I actually left work 30 minutes early in order to be sure I was on time for dinner. But on the way home my phone died, and I got stuck in a traffic jam caused by a horrible accident and so I didn't have any choice but to just sit there and wait. I hope you'll understand."

This example returns us to the issue of character raised in Chapter Four. The judgments we make about character are always connected to stories that narrate certain patterns of action. Or said differently, we rarely come to understand a particular virtue (such as faithfulness) by having someone give us a dictionary definition of it; rather, we come to understand such virtues by seeing them displayed and narrated in the lives of those around us.

A similar point can be made about the character of God as revealed in scripture. We come to understand the steadfastness of God as we read of ancient Israel's repeated rebelliousness and God's willingness to take them back. We come to understand something of the breadth of God's mercy as we read the story of Jonah and his mission to Israel's sworn enemies, the Ninevites. And we come to understand something of the depth of God's love as we follow Jesus on his way to the cross. In the same way, the gospels offer us not a list of abstract qualities Jesus possessed, but stories about his interactions with Pharisees and prostitutes, children and tax collectors. We know from the gospel accounts that Jesus's actions were open to more than one interpretation, just as ours are. How are we to understand his habit of eating with the wrong crowd? What are we to make of his seeming violations of the Sabbath? What was he doing when he overturned the tables of the moneychangers in the temple? The meaning of such actions is hardly self-evident. Not surprisingly, different interpretations of their meaning and significance often lead Christians to different conclusions about how best to follow him. Yet even when Christians have disagreed about some of these details, most have agreed we are called to pattern our lives after the character of Jesus as revealed through the stories of scripture.

One final point concerning how stories reveal character. If stories really are as central to understanding character as suggested above, then it should come as no surprise that Jesus himself often told stories. Stories grip our hearts and imaginations in ways abstract discourse usually doesn't. Good stories, moreover, are memorable in ways other forms of communication often are not. Jesus could have offered his hearers an elaborate theoretical discussion of the virtues of neighborly love; instead, he told the story of the Samaritan (Luke 10:25-37). Similarly, instead of presenting a philosophical discourse on the nature of God's love and mercy, he told the story of the prodigal son (Luke 15:11-32).

Perhaps all of the above will help us see that stories are rarely just stories, if by that we mean that stories are simply quaint ways of illustrating what could just as easily be ill by other means. On the contrary, stories are *the* primary way in which we make sense of our own lives and the lives of those around us.

Stories, Stories, Everywhere

As all of us are aware, scripture is not the only story around, nor are churches the only storytellers; rather, we are surrounded by powerful stories and storytellers. We are daily awash with voices telling us stories, offering to help us make sense of our lives. And as suggested above, these are never *just* stories but are also invitations to see in a certain way and to act in accordance with what we see.

For example, consider the different ways we are encouraged to think about ourselves and the world in light of the following kinds of stories:

- The stories our families tell about what it means to be a Smith, an Escobar, or a Chen.

- The stories teachers, politicians, and talk-show hosts tell about what it means to be a responsible citizen.

- The stories nearly everyone tells about how to be a good spouse, faithful friend, or reliable employee.

- The stories parents, friends, advertising, social media, and our favorite streaming services tell about what it means to be normal, successful, or beautiful.

- The stories communities of faith tell about who God is, what God is doing in the world, and who we are in light of both.

All these stories (and many more) don't fit together neatly into a single, meaningful narrative. And so we all elevate some stories above others, making some more central to how we understand ourselves and make sense of our lives in light of that more central story. But how does one story become more central or more important than others?

There's surely no single explanation for how this happens. Some people intentionally choose to make a particular story the lens through which they read and understand other stories; others feel as though a particular story chose them; still others find themselves working this out on an almost daily basis. But regardless of how it happens, the point is that all of us find ourselves trying to make sense of ourselves and the world through a complex web of stories that we have been told and which we subsequently retell ourselves and others.

A Fishy Story

Consider this story, excerpted from the book *A River Runs through It and Other Stories* by Norman Maclean:

In our family, there was no clear line between religion and fly fishing. We lived at the junction of great trout rivers in western Montana, and our father was a Presbyterian minister and a fly fisherman who tied his own flies and taught others. He told us about Christ's disciples being fishermen, and we were left to assume, as my brother and I did, that all first-class fishermen on the Sea of Galilee were fly fishermen and that John, the favorite, was a dry-fly fisherman.

It is true that one day a week was given over wholly to religion. On Sunday mornings my brother, Paul, and I went to Sunday school and then to "morning services" to hear our father preach and in the evenings to Christian Endeavor and afterwards to "evening services" to hear our

father preach again. In between on Sunday after-
noons we had to study The Westminster Shorter
Catechism *for an hour and then recite before we*
could walk the hills with him while he unwound
between services. But he never asked us more
than the first question in the catechism, "What is
the chief end of man?" And we answered together
so that one of us could carry on if the other forgot,
"Man's chief end is to glorify God, and to enjoy
Him forever." This always seemed to satisfy him,
as indeed such a beautiful answer should have,
and besides he was anxious to be on the hills
where he could restore his soul and be filled again
to overflowing for the evening sermon. His chief
way of recharging himself was to recite to us from
the sermon that was coming, enriched here and
there with selections from the most successful
passages of his morning sermon.

Even so, in a typical week of our childhood Paul
and I probably received as many hours of instruc-
tion in fly fishing as we did in all other spiritual
matters.

After my brother and I became good fishermen, we
realized that our father was not a great fly caster,
but he was accurate and stylish and wore a glove
on his casting hand. As he buttoned his glove in
preparation to give us a lesson, he would say, "It
is an art that is performed on a four-count rhythm
between ten and two o'clock."

After he buttoned his glove, he would hold his rod straight out in front of him, where it trembled with the beating of his heart. Always it was to be called a rod. If someone called it a pole, my father looked at him as a sergeant in the United States Marines would look at a recruit who had just called a rifle a gun.

My brother and I would have preferred to start learning how to fish by going out and catching a few, omitting entirely anything difficult or technical in the way of preparation that would take away from the fun. But it wasn't by way of fun that we were introduced to our father's art. If our father had had his say, nobody who did not know how to fish would be allowed to disgrace a fish by catching him.

My father was very sure about certain matters pertaining to the universe. To him, all good things—trout as well as eternal salvation—come by grace and grace comes by art and art does not come easy.

The stories we tell (and are told) about ourselves and our world are crucially important because they offer us whatever measure of coherence and meaning we find in life. They do this in part by offering us ways to tie together the disparate elements of our lives. If, for example, we tell a certain story about who we are and what life is about, it will not be surprising if we try to live into that story by cultivating certain desires, convictions and dispositions, engaging in certain practices, and making use of the power inherent in certain institutions. For example, many Americans have internalized cultural stories about the American Dream, upward socioeconomic mobility, and self-reliance. How deeply these narratives are ingrained will impact how a person understands their success or failure in the workplace, their relationships with their neighbors, financial choices, and more. For many Christians, there may be a felt tension between these cultural American stories and the story of our faith in Jesus.

Thus, an ongoing challenge for any faith community is to sort through the role stories play in its common life and in the lives of each disciple. What are the vital guiding stories a community of faith tells about itself? What stories does it tell about where it has been, where it is going, and how it cares for its neighbors? How has this congregation or parish come to understand itself in light of the story of scripture? And how does the community understand what God is doing in the world? As a congregation considers its desire for growth (or lack thereof), its ministry priorities, and its approach to building community, its members must first learn to recognize the stories they use to define what flourishing looks like for their church.

It may very well be that a significant part of being a disciple of Jesus Christ is the willingness and skill to read one's life—and the life of one's community of faith—through the story of "God-with-us" revealed in scripture and the history of the church. May God continue to shape us more fully into the image of Christ as we continue to be open to the transforming power of the Spirit working through that story.

Questions for Personal Reflection and Group Discussion

1. As you tell the story of your life, who are the most significant people? Why are these people so important in narrating who you are? What events over the course of your life do you tend to single out as most significant? Why have you come to see these as so important?

2. As you look to the future, what story do you see yourself living into? In other words, what story do you tell about where your life is headed? How is this story about your future connected to the story you tell about your past?

3. How does your congregation or parish tell its story? Are there certain people or events that are taken as central to the story? How and why? What story does your congregation hope to embody in the future?

4. What impact does the story of "God-with-us" as revealed in Scripture and church history have

on your own story and the story of your faith
community? In what ways does this Biblical story
inform or illuminate your self-understanding or
the identity of your community of faith?

Practices

Praise the LORD!
Praise God in his sanctuary;
praise him in his mighty firmament!
Praise him for his mighty deeds;
praise him according to his surpassing great-
ness!
Praise him with trumpet sound;
praise him with lute and harp!
Praise him with tambourine and dance;
praise him with strings and pipe!
Praise him with clanging cymbals;
praise him with loud crashing cymbals!
Let everything that breathes praise the LORD!
Praise the LORD!
–Psalm 150

Remember the sabbath day, and keep it holy. Six days you shall labor and do all your work. But the seventh day is a sabbath to the LORD your God; you shall not do any work—you, your son or your daughter, your male or female slave, your livestock, or the alien resident in your towns. For six days the LORD made heaven and earth, the sea, and all that is in them, but rested the seventh day; therefore the LORD blessed the sabbath day and consecrated it.
–Exodus 20:8-11

When an alien resides with you in your land, you shall not oppress the alien. The alien who resides with you shall be to you as the citizen among you; you shall love the alien as yourself, for you were aliens in the land of Egypt:
I am the Lord your God.
–Leviticus 19:33-34

...be kind to one another, tender-hearted, forgiving one another, as God in Christ has forgiven you.
–Ephesians 4:32

Practicing Faith

An important and potentially revolutionary shift is taking place in how many people think about the Christian faith. In the recent past, many

Christians assumed that what primarily marked them *as* Christians was that they held certain beliefs. (To connect this to an earlier chapter, we might say this way of identifying themselves as Christians was itself one of their central convictions about the Christian faith.) According to this way of thinking, a Christian is someone who, for example, believes Jesus was born of the virgin Mary, was the unique and only-begotten Son of God, was crucified to atone for our sins, and was resurrected by God on the third day. Not surprisingly, such an understanding of the Christian faith also led many to believe that what distinguished them from non-Christians (as well as from those in other Christian traditions) were primarily differences in what they believed.

As important as each of these beliefs are to the Christian faith, more and more Christians are rightly coming to see that beliefs alone do not define who they are as followers of Jesus. Equally central to this identity are certain *practices* of the Christian faith. Or perhaps put more accurately, practices are coming to be recognized as central to Christianity because practices are best understood as a kind of belief-in-action. Scripture is full of examples:

- Think of the many psalms or hymns found in scripture. It is one thing to believe intellectually that God is worthy of all praise; it is another to put that belief into practice by joyfully worshiping and offering God our praise.

- Consider God's commandment to keep the sabbath. Again, it is one thing to assent to the notion that God is sovereign and does not need our work to keep the world running; it is another to put that belief into practice by regularly resting from one's labors.

- Or recall God's instructions to ancient Israel concerning their treatment of foreigners in their land. Once again, it is one thing to affirm that we were exiles in a strange land and God took care of us; it's another to put that belief into practice *as the people of this God* by taking care of the strangers in our midst.

- Finally, it's one thing to assert that we have been forgiven by God; it's another to reflect the character of that God by putting this belief into action and forgiving those who have wronged us.

As these examples suggest, such practices serve both to express and reinforce basic convictions about who God is, what God does, and who God calls us to be. Over generations, engaging in such practices becomes not just a means to express convictions but also a means by which these convictions are formed in others. For example, children come to learn God is worthy of praise not only because they read it in scripture, but also because they are part of a community where God is worshiped and praised. Similarly, children come to learn that forgiveness is at the heart of the Christian faith not only because they are taught this or because they read it in scripture, but also because they are a part of a community where the practices of forgiveness and reconciliation are at the center of their common life.

Given that people hold a wide range of convictions and core beliefs, it's hardly surprising to discover that people engage in an equally wide range of practices and beliefs-in-action. Nor is it likely surprising to discover that practices are not just bound up with convictions, but also with desires and dispositions. But to begin to see some of these connections and to understand why any of this matters to discipleship, we need to back up once again and look more closely at how practices function in human life.

Practice, Practice, Practice

As noted above, when we speak of practices, we are referring to any activities we routinely engage in that *presume* and *reinforce* a particular way of life (with all its accompanying desires, convictions, virtues, etc.). As a kind of belief-in-action, practices flow from and bear witness to what people already believe about the world and their place in it, their desires and longings for the world and themselves, and the ways in which they are already disposed to interact in and with the world.

A relatively simple and mundane example may help clarify: the practice of washing your hands before a meal. The first and rather obvious thing to notice is that there's nothing natural about this practice; lots of people throughout history haven't washed their hands and plenty of people in the world today still don't. In short, people who wash their hands before they eat do so not because it's natural but because they have been formed over time to engage in this practice. The second thing to notice is that most of us no longer give much thought as to *why* we do it because it has become conventional wisdom, though the COVID-19 pandemic did raise the issue back to the front of our consciousness for a time. When the pandemic began, many of us suddenly became much more aware of our personal hygiene habits. Third, we should note that as children mature, they often come to understand better the reasons for handwashing and so come to make this practice their own, in the sense that they no longer see themselves as engaging in this practice primarily because their parents told them to.

But how is the practice of handwashing related to desires, convictions, and character? The connections become clearer when we ask ourselves some questions:

- What *desires* are presumed and reinforced by this practice? (The desire to be healthy and avoid illness; the desire to avoid spreading harmful germs to others; the desire to be seen as cultured or civilized.)

- What *convictions* are presumed and reinforced by this practice? (Convictions about what counts for good health; convictions about the means and likelihood of spreading disease; and convictions about the effectiveness of handwashing.)

- What *dispositions* or *virtues* are presumed and reinforced by this practice? (The disposition to act in our own best interest; the disposition to be considerate of the health and well-being of others; the disposition to act in ways that gain the approval and admiration of those around us; the virtue of doing something even though its desired effects are not immediately apparent.)

Finally, we should note that this practice is taught and reinforced by caretakers (and medical professionals) who tell stories of people who didn't practice good hygiene and became terribly sick. These stories, coupled with the above framework and our own sense of who our society holds up for commendation, go a long way toward giving us good reasons to wash our hands regularly.

The point here, of course, is not handwashing or the assumptions underwritten by such a practice. The only objective is to illustrate how a particular practice reinforces a whole range of ideas, many of which are subconscious. The recent COVID-19 pandemic further illustrated how the practices we do (or do not) engage in to remain healthy are often so normal and routine that we don't think carefully about them–until given good reason to. This is one of the primary reasons it's important to pay attention to the practices in which we engage. If something as simple as the practice of regularly washing your hands presumes and reinforces a whole set of desires, convictions, and dispositions, then it's quite possible we are daily being formed by all kinds of practices in which we engage but to which we pay very little attention.

Formative Practices

The practices that are most personally formative tend to be considerably more complicated than handwashing. To see this, take some time to reflect on the following list of everyday practices and see if you can discern some of the desires, convictions, and dispositions (as well as virtues and vices) that each practice likely presumes and reinforces:

- Making promises
- Planting and tending a garden
- Engaging in conversation
- Watching movies
- Saying you're sorry
- Praying
- Writing letters to a friend
- Singing a hymn with others
- Playing competitive sports
- Shopping for the latest fashions
- Taking walks in the woods or a park
- Recycling
- Scrolling on social media
- Voting in an election
- Visiting the elderly and the sick
- Taking a vacation
- Reading the Bible
- Sharing a meal
- Playing games with children

Each of the above practices—as well as nearly any practice that we could identify—could flow from very different ways of life. This observation has at least two important implications. First, it suggests that two people who *look* like they're doing the same thing may be better understood—at least for the reasons we care about here—as doing something very different. For example, a person who engages in a conversation primarily to hear their own voice is not doing the same thing as someone who engages in a conversation primarily to learn from another's perspective. Similarly, a person who reads the Bible because they enjoy reading ancient texts is not doing the same thing as someone who reads it expecting to be led by God. In short, the reasons we engage in a particular practice shape its formative effects.

It's not very instructive to simply *notice* a particular practice. What is always more important—and harder to get a handle on—is *why* a group of people engages in a particular practice in the first place. What does a community believe they are doing by engaging in a particular practice? This is only one reason why it's probably not particularly illuminating to count the number of people who engage in the practice of going to church each week, because what they understand themselves to be doing varies so greatly it hardly makes sense to say they are engaging in the same practice.

This leads directly to a second implication: The variety of *reasons* for engaging in a practice often lead to different *ways* of engaging in and evaluating it. A young man, for example, who regularly works out at the gym because he wants larger muscles is exercising (and evaluating his success) differently from someone who exercises to improve their health after a heart attack. Similarly, a woman who prays primarily to persuade God to provide what she desires is likely to engage in prayer differently (and evaluate its effectiveness differently) than someone who understands prayer primarily as aligning her desires with God's.

Potentially formative practices cannot be examined in isolation from the wider frameworks in which they are practiced. Engaging in particular practices, in other words, neither mechanically nor magically guarantees a particular outcome.

A Practical Example

In one local church, children were turning up an hour or more before the service, looking for company, entertainment, or mischief. Slowly congregants began to notice one explanation for the children's behavior was that they were hungry. So a pattern began of holding a breakfast 45 minutes before the service began, and during that time weaving into the conversation some high and low points in the week, encouragements and discouragements to faith, and hopes and fears for the near future. Gradually this breakfast extended to the whole congregation. Three or four times a year, instead of breakfast, everyone would set about getting ready for a celebratory lunch that would follow the service, and would be made up of contributions, great and small, from almost every member. Thus were human need and a point of aggravation transformed into an occasion of celebration, fellowship, and grace. The need of the human body became an experience of the body of Christ.[3]

In this brief account, we glimpse something of how practices are always situated in broader frameworks. Had this congregation been primarily motivated by desires for order or beliefs about who was responsible for these neighborhood children, they might have responded differently. Instead, the decision to begin a breakfast for these children was rooted in a whole set of convictions, stories, and other practices having to do with scripture's call to welcome the stranger and the church's experience of being fed at the Lord's Table by a generous and hospitable God. The *why* impacted the practices chosen, and the practices themselves continued to form the congregation into one that was increasingly hospitable, generous, and celebratory.

Practices Matter

Practices inevitably involve action, and every culture also tells us what will count for acting in the first place. In other words, every culture shapes us to think of certain things as "doing nothing." So, for example, if people in our day read Jesus's words about how we should respond when someone strikes us on the right cheek (Matthew 5:39),

---

[3] Wells, S. (2008). *God's Companions: Reimagining Christian Ethics.* Wiley-Blackwell.

our natural response, given the way we've been formed, is to ask, "But why does Jesus insist that I do nothing?" Of course, Jesus may not be asking us to do *nothing*, but to do the *harder* thing, which if you've ever done it, sure feels like you're doing *something*. A similar observation could be made regarding the practice of prayer, which many of us have come to think of as "not really doing anything."

Learning how practices form us is not easy. If it's any consolation, consider working through this material as itself a kind of practice—the practice of thinking hard about essential matters. Such a practice has its own rewards, though they rarely come quickly or easily. Pray that as you continue to think on these things and discuss them with others that God will help you see the ways in which the practices we engage in every day either help to fashion us more closely into the image of Christ or help to mold us into an image far less glorious.

Questions for Personal Reflection and Group Discussion

1. What practices do you regularly engage in that shape your view of the world? Take one of these specific practices and trace the possible connections between it and your convictions, desires,

and character. What story do you tell about why you engage in this practice?

2. What are some of the core practices at the center of your congregation's life together? To get at this, you might try filling in the following blank: "If we as a congregation or parish stopped [doing] _____, we would stop being who we are." What do those practices reflect about your community's convictions, desires, and character?

3. Once you have identified what you think are some of these core practices, reflect further on them by asking yourselves the following: How have each of these practices been nourished over time by our congregation? Have we changed how any of these practices are implemented over time? If so, how might these changes have altered how we are being formed?

4. Think about some Christian individuals or communities of faith with which you are familiar. Are there practices or disciplines that seem particularly important to them, but which are missing from your life or the life of your congregation? What do these differences suggest about your individual or shared desires, convictions, stories, and virtue? Are there changes you wish to make in what and how you practice?

Institutions

You shall observe this rite as a perpetual ordinance for you and your children. When you come to the land that the LORD will give you, as he has promised, you shall keep this observance. And when your children ask you, "What do you mean by this observance?" you shall say, "It is the passover sacrifice to the LORD, for he passed over the houses of the Israelites in Egypt, when he struck down the Egyptians but spared our houses."
–Exodus 12:24-27

Then [Jesus] said to them, "The sabbath was made for humankind, and not humankind for the sabbath."
–Mark 2:27

For I received from the Lord what I also handed on to you, that the Lord Jesus on the night when he was betrayed took a loaf of bread, and when he had given thanks, he broke it and said, "This is my body that is broken for you. Do this in remembrance of me." In the same way he took the cup also, after supper, saying, "This cup is the new covenant in my blood. Do this, as often as you drink it, in remembrance of me." For as often as you eat this bread and drink the cup, you proclaim the Lord's death until he comes.
—1 Corinthians 11:23-26

When you hear the word *institution*, what images come to mind? Do you find the associations conjured by this word largely positive or negative? If you're like a lot of folks in contemporary society, you are somewhat suspicious, if not distrustful, about the role of institutions in human life and the power they often wield. Author Yuval Levin summarizes many years of data on this issue: "In the early 1970s, 80 percent of Americans told Gallup they had 'a great deal' or 'quite a lot' of confidence in doctors and hospitals, for instance. In 2018, the figure was 36 percent. Forty years ago, 65 percent of Americans said they had 'a great deal' or 'quite a lot' of confidence in organized religion, while in 2018 just 38 percent did. Sixty percent expressed confidence in the public schools back then, while just 29 percent did so in 2018. Even in 1975, a year after Richard Nixon's resignation in disgrace, 52 percent of

Americans expressed confidence in the presidency, while in 2018 just a third of Americans did. Gallup found that 42 percent of the public had confidence in Congress in the 1970s. In 2018, that figure stood at a stunningly low 11 percent." Some of this distaste may spring from the impersonal character of institutions, while some may spring from a deep reservoir of stories all of us can tell about corrupt, coercive, and oppressive institutions, including some (such as slavery) which were designed that way from the beginning. Indeed, many people held up as heroes in our collective memory—Harriet Tubman, Mahatma Gandhi, Nelson Mandela, Martin Luther King, Jr., Rosa Parks—are typically regarded *as* heroes precisely because they stood up against unjust and oppressive institutions. We also hear echoes of the more general suspicion of all institutions when people consider themselves to be spiritual but have little interest in or respect for the so-called "institutional church."

Dealing Head-on with Our Bias

Despite the cultural distrust of institutions, our daily lives are shaped and ordered—often for the better—by countless institutions. In what follows, we will use a rather broad definition of *institution*. For our purposes in this field guide, an institution is any organization or social structure that orders life for a particular group of people.

In addition to those organizations we typically think of when we think of institutions, this broader definition includes agencies, laws, traditions, programs, policies, committees, etc.! Institutions are created to serve (and preserve) a way of life some people regard as worthy of being sustained. At their best, institutions enable the passing down of wisdom, knowledge, and a way of life from one generation to another. Consider a brief list of some contemporary institutions that directly and indirectly shape our lives:

- Educational institutions: schools, colleges, universities, accrediting associations, libraries

- Political institutions: political offices, elections, rule of law, founding documents (constitutions, etc.)

- Legal institutions: legislatures, laws, courts, police departments, prisons

- Medical institutions: hospitals, medical schools, insurance regulations

- Social and cultural institutions: marriage, family, language, holidays, traditions, museums, entertainment industries

- Economic institutions: businesses and industries, currencies, banks, stock and bond markets, labor unions, regulatory agencies

At least four important things are worth considering when reviewing such a list. First, every institution is the result of shared convictions concerning what is important in human life. For example, it's precisely because many people share convictions about the relationship between knowledge, its dissemination, and the public good that we have such institutions as public libraries.

Second, the boundaries between different categories of institutions (educational, legal, medical, etc.) are relatively arbitrary and fluid, because many of these institutions could easily be placed in more than one category. For instance, the entertainment industry functions both as a social and an economic institution, and arguably as an educational one as well. (For those wondering about the absence of so-called "religious institutions" from the list, rest assured this omission was intentional. See question #3 below.)

Third, despite the distrust many understandably have against some institutions, it's difficult to imagine human life without them. In fact, it's not clear that humans could do without institutions even if we wanted to. We seem drawn to creating structures that seek to bring a measure of order out of chaos and extend a particular way of life across generations.

Finally, it's not clear we *should* want to do without many of our institutions, for despite their shortcomings and potential for being twisted to false purposes, institutions often support cooperation and flourishing within and across diverse populations that few of us would be willing (or wise) to give up, such as social and cultural institutions like the arts, public schools, or a free press.

So at the end of the day, alongisde the reservations we might have about certain institutions, most of us are probably glad there are laws about which side of the street to drive on and disincentives for breaking those laws. Most of us likely appreciate there are hospitals to care for our loved ones and agencies that regulate what can be put in our food and drinking water. And most of us are probably grateful that we can read these chapters and reflect on them seriously, having been schooled in the art of reading and thinking carefully.

The Purpose of Institutions

Although institutions and structures come into existence in lots of different ways, they almost always take the form they do in order to support and sustain practices, desires, convictions, and the like. For example, people throughout history have thought it important to educate their young, though the means and structures they employed to accomplish this have varied widely. Local public school systems represent one such set of structures and institutions, and they reflect and reinforce a whole set of desires, convictions, dispositions, and practices.

We have left the issue of institutions in our discussion of formation for the last chapter not because they are less important than the other aspects, but because institutions make so little sense *apart* from the other aspects. In other words, institutions are structures that directly and indirectly flow out of, instill, and support certain sets of desires, convictions, virtues, stories, and practices. For these reasons, *institutions are inherently formative in character.*

Take, for example, an institution from the list above. To understand this institution *as* an institution and as inherently formative, consider each of the following questions:

- What desires are met, instilled, and validated in and through this institution (and the practices it supports)?

- What convictions lead people to believe a particular institution is necessary or at least desirable? What (and whose) agreed-upon and shared purposes does it supposedly serve?

- What dispositions, inclinations, and virtues, and vices does this institution nurture, both intentionally and unintentionally?

- What stories are told about why this institution exists and why it holds its current shape?

- What practices does this institution support and make possible? How does the current shape of this institution influence how these practices are executed?

Whatever sense we make of institutions cannot be easily separated from how we understand these other aspects of our lives. Moreover, as noted above, whatever hesitation or suspicion we may have about institutions cannot be linked simply to their character as institutions, for as such they support and maintain much of what we rightly care about. So what is it about institutions that makes us so nervous?

A Life of Their Own

Most institutions are very much like ocean liners: They're hard to turn on a dime. In other words, institutions can change course, but not easily and typically not very quickly. For this reason alone, institutions tend to be conservative in nature. This does, of course, have a positive side: by their very character as institutions, these structures are bigger than—and therefore should be outside the easy control or manipulation of—solitary individuals. But the potential downside is that over time, institutions can take on a life of their own, often independent of the purposes they were brought into existence to serve. When this happens, people often care more deeply about preserving certain institutional structures than about whether these structures still serve the purposes for which they were created.

For example, the popular school calendar, which gives students two or three months off in the summer, was instituted long ago when many families were involved in agriculture and needed their children home to help during the busy growing season. Since that time, much has changed, and some school districts have instituted a different school calendar tied more closely to educational purposes and current cultural realities. But as debates across the country have shown, changing an institutional form like the school calendar is no easy task.[4] Even though most children are no longer directly involved in agriculture, the rhythm of their lives has been formed by a calendar that was instituted as though they were. Over time, people began to think of the summer months less as a time for farming and more as a time for family vacations.

---

[4] Morin, Amanda. (2024, July 23). *The Pros and Cons of Year-Round School.* Parents. https://www.parents.com/year-round-schooling-schedule-pros-cons-8661943

As a result, the school calendar now serves different purposes than it was designed to serve. Whether those purposes are just as worthy of being served, or whether some other purposes ought to take center stage, is really what current debates are about.

Of course, concerns about institutions taking on a life of their own are nothing new. Jesus himself seemed to have his own concerns regarding the institution of the sabbath. According to scripture, God instituted the sabbath to provide rest from the toil and anxiety of everyday life. By the time of Jesus, however, the sabbath had taken on a life of its own. Indeed, the purpose of the sabbath seemed to have been turned on its head: People devoted enormous amounts of energy trying to follow all the well-intentioned rules designed to help people know whether or not they were keeping the sabbath. One of the unintended consequences of such rule-following is an inevitable anxiety about keeping the various sabbath rules. Like Laura Ingalls Wilder in *The House in the Big Woods,* those attempting to keep the sabbath were often eager for it to be over. So rather than being a respite from toil and anxiety, the sabbath had become a new source of both!

It's tempting to look at this situation and assure ourselves we would never do something like that. But are we so sure? Each of us is likely being shaped by institutions that seem so natural in their current form, so much a part of the fabric of everyday life as we have come to experience it, that we have long ago stopped (or perhaps never even started) asking about those institutions' purposes. For example, Wendell Berry has tried for decades to generate a national discussion about what we call "the economy," insisting it's impossible to have a good economy unless we're much clearer than we are about the purposes it's supposed to serve. Likewise, Neil Postman has asked similar questions about public education, suggesting that what we most need in our country is not a debate about national testing or putting more computers in classrooms but a frank and honest discussion about the purposes public education is supposed to serve.

So What's the Church For?

Perhaps it's also time for followers of Jesus in our day to ask similar questions about the church and its institutional form and structures. In our day, there are many proposals on offer for how to do church better, but perhaps what is most needed is a frank and open discussion about God's purpose for the church. Does it really make sense to evaluate these various contemporary proposals for improving church apart from examining the purposes church is supposed to serve? Do we know what those purposes are? Do we know whether or to what extent our faith community as it is currently organized is fulfilling those purposes?

The church is often described as a collection of people who have something in common–the Christian faith–and who get together regularly to share it with each other and to communicate it to those outside. This understanding of the church is a clearly articulated purpose and may seem reasonable. But such an understanding does not do justice to the New Testament's vision of the church. In scripture we learn the church is not so much a host site for like-minded individuals as it is a people who are called out in order to *see* more truthfully—God, God's creation, and themselves—and who are called to be a sign and witness to God's redemptive purposes for the world. In his well-known book *Life Together*, German theologian Dietrich Bonhoeffer rightly insisted the church "is not an ideal which we must realize; it is rather a reality created by God in Christ in which we may participate." Understood this way, the church is not an *institution* to be managed by smart people but a communion across time and space, whose purpose is to worship and bear witness to the God revealed through God's covenantal relationship with ancient Israel and the life, death, and resurrection of Jesus Christ.

Questions for Personal Reflection and Group Discussion

1. What structures and institutions influence the shape of your daily life? In what specific ways do these structures and institutions exert their influence? Where are you thankful for the ordering and influence these structures bring? Where (and why) are you frustrated by these structures and institutions?

2. As you've thought about institutions in light of this conversation, what examples have you come up with of institutions or structures that may have taken on a life of their own and now no longer serve the purposes for which they were brought into being?

3. Not only does every culture order the lives of its citizens by means of certain institutions (such as legal and economic structures), but every culture also forms us to understand the relationship among different institutions in certain ways. For example, the church is widely believed to be an institution charged with addressing the religious or spiritual concerns of its members as opposed to their educational, economic, legal or political concerns, which are handled by other institutions. What do you see as the advantages and disadvantages of this division of labor?

4. Reflect on the institutional structure of your faith community and the broader church

structures to which it belongs. In your view, where do the current institutional structures foster genuine growth and discipleship and how? Where do they possibly inhibit growth and discipleship? Can you imagine different structures or institutions that might better serve the purposes of the church as you understand them?

Conclusion

A human body thrives and moves through the world by means of an ongoing conversation of all its parts. When a person is young and immature, the parts of their body don't yet know how to communicate well with one another and to work together. A young person also doesn't have a fully developed sense of the external forces—like gravity—that bear down on their body.

Similar dynamics are at play in our churches, as manifestations of Christ's body in their particular locations. We often don't have a full sense of all the members God has gathered in our congregation. Additionally, we often have a fuzzy sense of our identity and of the forces that guide and shape us. The chapters in this book provide us with language and concepts to orient us on our journey toward maturity as a body, but they are just a starting place. We must put them in action in our churches, as we work to discern who we are as communities of God's people. Understanding the shape of our congregational lives will help us discern what faithfulness to the way of Jesus looks like for us, teaching us how to pay attention to dynamics that unfold among us and around us.

A nature lover's experience of the outdoors will be far richer if she knows the names and habits of the birds, wildflowers, or other creatures she encounters in her neighborhood. What song belongs to which bird? Which flower will bloom in July? A field guide serves to train one's attention, and in the process to deepen one's love for its subject. We hope that this field guide will be one you return to often, training your attention to many key facets of life together in a church community and deepening your love for the church and our Creator.

Appendix: Scripture for Further Study

Our hope for this book is that it will be useful in your specific church context, as clergy and lay leaders guide congregations in spiritual formation. While scripture has been referenced throughout the book, this appendix compiles a few suggestions for Bible passages related to the themes and content of each chapter. These scriptures might prove helpful in writing sermons about these topics or could be employed at the beginning or end of small group meetings to frame the discussion.

Chapter One: Formation Happens!

- Psalm 1
- Luke 2:40
- 1 Corinthians 3

Chapter Two: Desires

- Psalm 84
- Hosea 6:4-6 (with echoes in Matthew 9:13 and 12:7)
- Galatians 5:16-17

Chapter Three: Convictions

- Deuteronomy 6:4-9
- Daniel 1
- Mark 8:27-30

Chapter Four: Character

- John 15
- Ephesians 4-5
- James 1:22-27

Chapter Five: Stories

- Deuteronomy 4:1-40
- Luke 24:13-35
- Acts 7

Chapter Six: Practices

- Deuteronomy 6:16-25
- Proverbs 22
- Matthew 5:1-7:29

Chapter Seven: Institutions

- Ezra 1
- Romans 13:1-7
- 1 Peter 2:13-17

About the Authors

Philip D. Kenneson has taught for over three decades at Milligan University where he teaches the capstone course for all seniors. He has also been part of The Ekklesia Project from the beginning and for over two decades has served in several leadership roles, including as the Director of the Congregational Formation Initiative.

Debra Dean Murphy is Professor of Religious Studies and Co-Director of the Center for Restorative Justice at West Virginia Wesleyan College. She is the author of *Teaching That Transforms: Worship as the Heart of Christian Education* (Wipf & Stock), *Happiness, Health, and Beauty: The Christian Life in Everyday Terms* (Cascade). Her current research and writing interests center on climate grief and radical hope.

Rev. Jenny C. Williams is a United Methodist clergyperson who served local churches for over 20 years. She co-founded the West Virginia Faith Collective, a group of faith-based organizations doing justice and advocacy work in the state, and currently serves as the Faith Organizer for the ACLU of West Virginia.

Stephen E. Fowl is President and Dean of the Church Divinity School of the Pacific. A scholar of the New Testament, he has published numerous books and articles on the relationships between scriptural interpretation and the Christian life. Steve is an Episcopal lay person.

James W. Lewis is Dean Emeritus of the Anderson University School of Theology and Christian Ministry, where he taught for 24 years. He currently serves as the Senior Pastor of the South Park Church of God in southeast Houston.

Thanks for reading!

If you enjoyed this book, please leave a review at Amazon or your favorite online retailer.

Forthcoming from Englewood Press:

The Virtue of Dialogue: Becoming a Thriving Church through Conversation
by C. Christopher Smith

The Generosity of God's People: Economic Practice in the Local Church
by Kelly Johnson
(tentative title)

Connect with the Englewood Review of Books:

Website: englewoodreview.org
Facebook: facebook.com/erbks
Instagram: instagram.com/erbooks
X: x.com/erbks

Made in the USA
Columbia, SC
26 November 2024

47586979R00076